FIVE ASPECTS

AKIRA

PAXTON & BARKER
A SKILLPOINT IMPRINT

ISBN 978-9949-01-678-5

Dear Reader,

The words on these pages are for you,

to hold in your heart, to cherish, to love,

to share, to sing and dance and shout,

to give comfort in your time of need.

Let no one tell you how to live.

Let no one tell you who you can love.

CONTENTS

DREAMING — 1

LONGING — 37

BEING — 73

LASTING — 115

CHANGING — 151

DREAMING

AKIRA

—

1

I hear you there

in my thoughts

tending advice,

as if I'd heard

your sweet voice

the night before

the morning flash,

the breeze in my hair,

the twinge of sunshine

that stings my face.

I awaken to the light

and look up to the sun,

glowing in the heavens,

to try and catch a glimpse

of your face once again.

I chase you in my dreams,
like a young songbird away.
I chase you in the evening,
and at midnight you are gone.

As the lights are burning low
I still chase the one I love, for
while the world is breaking fast
I cannot come to my nest again,
until you are beside me once more.

When I remember you, it is as

a dream of yesterday, a clear vision

that through the darkness of the past,

like some strange song, seems to me

come from some forgotten heart of old.

And in the silence of the moonlight

my own heart murmurs, and you speak,

for through this dream of mine you seem

as you have never truly ever been before,

a shining angel bearing love and hope.

The rapture of joy and pain,

the gentleness and respect of age,

the tenderness and faith of youth.

I felt your light sweet breathing,

and your free, soft words to me,

and saw in your smiling eyes,

your warm heart, kind and true.

Love spreads its wings
and climbs the air,
it seizes every wind,
it sighs and laughs,
shakes the heights,
and throws itself down.

All these visions

of my early dreams

shall soon all seem to be

but mimicked fires, which

in the flames of early love,

played the same false tune.

Softly swimming
to the waves below,
slim, youthful fancies
float around me,
sly is my heart
and restless my brow,
for someone is with me,
here in the moonlight.

Leaning on the prow
and her whispering low,
I turn back my thoughts
to where I stand now,
and the young woman
who is looking at me
draws me to the deep,
into her cold embrace.

The kiss of a fay
of your sweet lips
whom my heart-strings
like a lute have wove.

Of your tender hands
white lilies they clasp
as kisses sweet as violets
soothe my raging heart.

The feel of you atop my chest

as I slumber and rest with you,

so soft, so soft, my kisses fall,

so tender, so tender, their kiss,

when I wrap you with my arms

you are in the clasp of my love.

XX

Forgive me if I shut my eyes and dream,

and feel the warm heat of your body press

against my own, your lips meeting mine,

my heart ever beating faster and louder

with the world standing all before me.

Gazing up at the moon
with wonder on her face,
till in her bright silver glory
she hides in the high heavens
all the treasures of a wide sky.

And as my gaze is fixed I do see,
reflected in the golden sunlight,
eclipsing a heaven of great stars,
the image of her, shining bright,
full of love, and hope for the day.

With we once more in our clothes
we walked out in the cold again
in some dim alley, cold and dull,
and felt the rain and the wind,
as we curled up in the dark.

All the while I gazed as I
heard the icy rain falling
on the cheeks of an angel,
and the beauties of my life
they grew clearer and clearer,
her echo growing ever stronger,
wandering about me in my dreams,
haunting me for the days to come.

On from the heavens I will go, and out

along the rolling green fields by the sea,

the heart of a dim sky where my love lies.

For she is still but a stranger to this land,

and whilst her heart may still be troubled,

I am resolved to take all her pains away.

In the wooded vale her face

so sweetly smiled upon my sight,

as the moon in heaven sublime

lay with a silver crest overhead,

together we shared in its light,

bound as one under the stars.

Shining through your lucid robe

the countenance of an angel's hue,

who my rude and rough hands did guide

to your soft pillow, upon a cloud of bliss.

How long shall your charms linger

and how long will your spell last,

for all day and night in vain I seek

to find the one who bound me fast.

The silks upon your shoulders,
the pearl-drops in your eyes,
and a faint, distinct perfume
from the fragrant roses.

It softly drifts from a meadow,
and there, in the distant trees,
over you, and under you,
the silver of your hair.

There it hangs on your cheek,
a sworn, solemn promise,
a true, eternal vow that
we will be together again.

My fair-haired buttercup,

such pure beauty you wear,

dainty and sweet-breasted,

virtuous, fair and slender,

and always rushing to be

by a handsome lad seen.

I love you more dearly than I can tell
for life within your arms is all anew,
my heart enclosed within your embrace
where you safely take me to your domain,
as all of our worldly cares wash away.

I hear your singing in my dreams
my sweetheart love, lone and fair,
and with the music of your voice,
of your clear, honey-laden hymns.

The hymns that draw me beside you,
to the banks of our childhood river,
to listen to the swift rushing waters
as they thrill and sweep, and flutter,
holding you within their embrace.

I hear your soft, tender voice

calling me to rest in my chamber,

afar from the west like a glorious sun.

A wonder like the northern lights enkindled,

the love-note of your holy song, and my words

become lost, like single threads of golden straw,

your call in my heart, and your heart in my voice.

In the coming years, my love,

when the bridal bed is spread

with a touch of summer's day,

I shall watch you softly sleep

while the scarlet is in your hair,

and the roses show on your cheeks,

with the petunias by the porch

whispering of your bridal joy.

The stars taught
my love of words,
but you are now
the shining gem
that comforts me.

A brilliant light,
hanging above me,
guiding my dreams.

I cannot see the end, but I can feel

the lovely warmth of your arms again.

I cannot see the sky, but my soul can feel

your pure, perfect eyes, whereon I sink.

I follow where your spirit leads,

for I know that you keep us whole.

The breeze from the lonely isles blowing

over our heads like a blanket of snow,

thick, yet suffocating with icy grip.

They parted us, as leaves in the autumn,

and my aching heart, as I lie here, floated away,

to join you with the morning stars, up in the sky.

I see the brilliant stars in your eyes,

just as they are reflected in the sea,

and the whole world is as if it were

a stairway, made for you to descend,

leading to all the joys we will share.

She was as perfect as she could be,

perfect in so far as to reign my heart,

a dream from within my very soul.

A nobleness that made her stoic and wise,

her very poise defining grace and charm,

a keen mind that knew no malice or ill,

and a boundless heart, open to share.

We wandered far from the halls of love,

we faced the rain and the bitter wind,

yet I wait until you find me once more,

to tell me our dream is true and good.

The girl whom I love
looks down at me,
with eyes fixed
her lips set apart,
full of joy, of kisses,
as I move to her embrace.

Sit and rest your head,

there upon my shoulder,

as you read your books,

and draw on your maps,

dreaming of daring tales

of bravery and adventure.

Stay here until your gaze

rests upon the mountains,

and reaches out at last

in peace and wonder.

LONGING

I seek you with a touch of desire,

the feeling is one that will not pass,

the thought is not, and shall not be,

of any death, or frequent change.

I touch you, and as a young man

I seem and am not what you see,

I strive, I soar, I drink, and pass

out of the world we held so dear.

My tender soul longs for you so,

longing for you to proudly soar above,

leaving behind the world of men

and all its chattering cares.

All my life I've run away from love
and have sought the rich woods alone,
and walked by many a winding stream
that tell tales of a forgotten coast.

Yet I still remember your dear name
and ever remember your sweet words,
every summertime when skies are blue
and the trees whisper in the shade.

Led by the breath of your perfume,

and lost in the silence of your eyes,

whose colour or warmth never fades,

and whose heart is not still or drowned.

Pleasure, with her ardent grace,

with her rare, golden, silken hair.

Pleasure, in her warm embrace,

her hand by flowing waters hung.

Pleasure, a green and golden earth,

of all sweetest leaves and flowers,

her flowing locks and gentle touch.

Pleasure, in the bosom of the brook,

where she smiles with joy and love.

Pleasure of the forest's life, she makes,

that whose life is heaven-like true.

The light on your lips
and the glint in your eye,
that I should still be yours,
yet you are not my own.

That your heart as mine
should mine be yours,
to give you endless love
with no hint of regret.

From the secret flowery meadow,

pressing with her tender fingers,

on the verdant forest branches,

gently moving along the trees,

warming nature with her heat.

The stars indeed behold her kindly,

and on the sunbeam gently falling,

she alights upon the silver lake,

and on it's brink she rests her head,

in the cool, refreshing breeze.

As I look towards you,

I feel myself grow small.

I fear to stand in front of you,

to look you in the face.

I fear you may well turn back,

and say nothing can touch you.

I fear that I might rise and fall,

in love with you in a moment's space.

When you were my every waking thought

each moment apart was as if it was a long year,

my consciousness consumed, as yours was too.

Yet as I look, and as I dream, you are still there

again by my side, as I lay with a tear in my eye,

as the thoughts of you come to me again.

Remember the day when we first met
and the music of the roaring chase,
your blue eyes, so wild and bright,
and your cheeks, searing hot with joy.

I long for those days once more my love,
yet they remain locked away, in memory.

I have loved and missed so long, you

who have grown with me as dearest lover,

whose voice has struck through me,

and who has always had such tender eyes,

and so much gentleness and grace.

My heart and yours shall be ever true,

so let us live, forgetting everything

and singing forever as we used to sing,

our griefs, our fears, forgetting them all,

our hands joined tightly until the end.

I sat upon the mountainside,
and gazed upon the clouds that flew
over the glittering mountain's mazed floor.

And there, between two grand towers
there you sat, elegantly dressed in pure white
with a look so divine, touched by a hint of rose
flushing over your cheeks, down your shoulders,
sitting beside the tall pines with alluring eyes,
tempting me down to join you in glee.

I long to feel your love
and see your beauty,
to hear your voice
as you would sing it.

To see the yellow-crimson of sunset
glowing within your dusky eye,
upon your darkened ruby lips.

To dream again of nights when we were bound,
when our passion and lustfulness was shared,
and of your fair face that no other knew,
that hid such loving warmth and care.

I feel your warmth, and the soul of me
is filled with a tender sweetness and light.

I sit by your side, and watch, and wait
to know how you will answer my heart's kiss.

Her rosy cheeks are in my thoughts
and it's very sweet to think,
I'm somewhere so very close to her
and the brilliant light of day.

But oh, that longing and that pang
when she finds herself departing,
as if the skies above were being drowned.

I long to turn, and catch a final glimpse.

If I gave you only three words,

you would say them to me, I know,

and you would make them into a song,

and I would live my life at peace again.

In an older life of ease and joy,

I would work for my lady's hand,

to raise her up to happiness,

and I'd wish to be glad to know

no evil could come of my love.

I'd wish of no ill thought to mar

the days that are bright and fair,

and wish her youth's soft glow

to have only cheerful measure, and

I'd wish no love that would not be,

in her kind and loving embrace.

She sees not a world
with its troubles and ills,
nor is vexed with care
of worldly comforts.

Instead she sits, and sings,
and dances, and laughs,
till all her life seems
a merry, jocund jest,
with all her admirers,
as puppets on a string,
longing to share with her
a taste of her true freedom.

Your gracious, beautiful lips once more
kissed my empty heart with softness pure.

You taught us, with no shyness or doubt,
how we could love, how well we could cherish,
unearthing the deepest secrets of our souls.

Warmly you lie there as in a nest,

your curls resting as soft as the snow,

when winter is upon us, cold and bitter,

with not a single leaf in all the barren trees,

and you smile at me, my fair one, as sweet

as the dew that the morning kisses give,

while you hold me fast and lull me back,

back into your tender warm embrace.

I ask not for your gentle smile to guide

my steps at night, nor ask you to be mine.

I only would be yours, and with your love

remember the days that sent my heart to you.

Your love is as great as your spirit,

but my heart feels as small as a bee,

that is flying up against your windows,

aimless and lost, looking for its home.

Our souls are

innocent

as is your love,

unblemished

by a thought

of sin or blame,

and though my soul

is troubled by fear,

my breath made

spirit-pulsing

by your air,

I think of you,

for I must think of you,

as fresh and sweet as any flower I see,

as pure as the silent dews of night,

and as a love that has no name.

I remember the nightgown you wore,

whose silken folds softly leaned to rest

upon your form as my quiet hands caressed,

and in their faint, pleasant touch, explored

a delicate body protecting a tender soul,

one that wove our spirits into a mantle,

enclosing us in a magic sense of warmth.

At the sight of you I grow more love-stricken,

with a force more than the fierce mountain winds

that war with one another across the alpine peaks,

for I am besieged by the sweet perfume of your scent,

and as I write for you, I feel the joy of your name

shine in all the corners of my heart and soul.

When the sun comes
along the rough valley track
and I think I see you, how glad I am,
to have you in my sight, to reach out far
and tightly hold your hand in the country
where you strayed so free, now proudly there
you ride and play, if only ever for one brief day.

Lifting in tender guise her face,

a form of grace and beauty fair,

with round green eyes and a smile,

as though she wished it be known

that her heart was only filled by love.

You enchant as you move across the room,

a singular sight, in spite of all tradition,

and when we've had our sprightly hours

and they all cease to be, I will still complain

that I must dearly wait to witness you again.

I am forever

living in the past,

while a burning fire

that keeps my love alive,

rages in my heart for all time,

aching to be with her once again.

BEING

Her heart was all too wide for me,

and I might never have reached out

to feel her love, or lifted up my

thoughts to touch her heart again,

were it not for her warm embrace.

I remember the red maple

and the tall silver-lined birch,

the golden hazel, shining bright

where the wild strawberries grow.

And all that long summer we knew

the meadow flowers of the earth,

the deep crimson roses of the sky,

I send these all to you, my love.

Your kisses fall
    and deeply burn,
To singe my heart
    with such a heat.

And from our love
    the wild desire,
To cling and grasp,
    to stay in our den.

On my heart you are always fluttering,
which always brings me hope and comfort,
and even when alone, you warm me gently
with your ever bright and loving gaze.

Love can be a most painful drug,
if not handled with utmost care.

Yet when I once more look on
upon the lovely face I love,
every nerve in my breast
ties in, and holds her fast,
till heart and mind both agree
that we shall live and love at last.

Your love burns inside me
like a phoenix rising, rekindled,
and yet all I know is where
that love-lorn bird is flying,
to find your fiery nest again
and not be turned to ash.

Gaze up at the stars,

for our destiny is bound

into the vast great unknown,

where we were joined as one,

for all the winds that blow,

ours is the wind of love.

As I explore you with my silver tongue,
I feel your body burn, and tremble and ache,
with that great love which never is forgot.

Such love I had from you, and with my hands,
kissed every inch, and always will I caress,
your delicate hands, your softened touch.

We lie in wait for love today

and all the world is waiting for us,

but we like to wander, you and I.

To roam, as children roam about

through the same common air,

we like to wander, you and I,

in love and peace of mind.

This love is the swiftest,

the sweetest, and the fairest.

The rosy lips that I kissed,

they are so warm and kind,

so bright and true, so pure.

Never a heart that's as whole

and full of loving kindness

will I ever meet or know again.

You and I had laughed a hundred times,

and once more we would sit and chat,

and I would think of the coming kiss,

and you would smile, and we'd both lie

together, thankful for our good fortune.

I love the sound of your sweet singing,

no mortal ever heard a sound so pure,

and though I alone gaze upon your form

with all the world before you, you stand,

acting as the sunshine of all human joys.

Your crimson lips, your soft embrace
lurking within your tangled hair,
and your eyes, they circle me, watching,
knowing that I may have my satisfaction.

From the emerald grass I see you gently passing,

I see the sun on your cheeks, reflected in the dew

and I know we could not be happier than today,

at the fountain of pools where all the roses glow,

where the flowers twine and the air sings its song.

All the world seems
yours to conquer,
and my heart grows
sweet again with you.

My eyes then fill with
the blessings of love,
and I thank my soul
for the honest wealth,
of all your loving care
and its many rewards.

I belong to you and you alone,

so by this token, my heart must be

restored to the tender care of you,

to keep me all at one with your own.

I will remember always

the deepest vow of my heart,

and this is my oath, that ever

from day to day I will kiss you,

I will love you, long for you,

for my maid and my love,

till the darkness is fled,

and that our lives shall be

as bright as our first morn.

I love you for the light of your eyes,

for the words which your voice bears,

and for the love that is in your heart.

I love you for all your virtuous deeds,

for the reassuring charm of your smile,

and for the grace that you carry your form.

I love you for all your many other gifts,

for the ones you share as a generous soul,

and for the ones you keep reserved for me.

When out of the distance

I see you as you softly smile,

as if the evening was beautiful

and the fair day had just begun,

causing me to rise, to stir once more,

renewed with vigor, seeking your light.

I know that there is something more

than song and laughter and the sun,

something more than beauty or renown,

and something more than all those things,

shines through in your compassion and grace.

Coiled like snakes

we writhe and squirm,

we twist and shrink

as on a string.

Like birds in prison

we lie in wait,

in our bliss,

with our heads

towards the ground.

I have always loved the shape of you,

the form of your neck and your shoulders,

the way you wore that elegant, purple dress.

The vain men who stand nearby in awe

have never truly seen your fairest form,

that of your voice and your singing,

your sage words and attentive care,

that of your tender, loving embrace.

The love you now are freely giving

will never cease to warm my heart,

not a night, not a day, not a week

will pass without a thought of you,

so radiant, so kind and so sweet,

like a dream that never will end.

I love you most of all,

when you look from your pillow,

that faint smile of joy and calm,

as the summer sun is sinking low,

creeping through the garden trees,

as the clouds are slowly parting,

like ripples in a quiet lake.

When my eyes land upon her

my spirit and my soul are as one,

for the charms within the range of her

are blended so well, in such alike a manner

as to make them seem all like one another,

a pure, elemental creature, the one I love.

Not a moment will I forget
the love we shared last night,
and now the day is dawning
with the first faint glimmer
of a crimson, rising sun,
I wish for it to flee again,
to leave us in the dark.

Fixing the glance of your keen eyes,

marking the music of your sighs,

you fill my soul with much delight

for every note that you do sing.

We in our joy are happier than

any brave hero or heroine, as if we

learned in classical tales of heroics,

that we know how much more fair

in our deep and true everlasting love

our humble selves did fully become.

You stand beside me
with your eyes fixed on the sea.

The leaves are on fire,
the morning stars are in the sky.

As the sun slowly rises in the east
you look, you behold in the western sky,
of the heavens in dusk and twilight white,
your hands in mine, our kisses burning hot.

I love watching you move the way you do,

at most this evening before the stars of night,

knowing at morn you'll wake up at my side

in the same slow, confident, comforting way.

You look into my eyes as if I held

some grand old spirit of the world's desire,

or secrets I might come to know some other day,

but all I wonder is what your eyes can see,

what your thoughts can tell, and what

your soul's imagination can convey.

Over mountain, and over lake and land

when first your quill did the ocean paint,

when the breeze did your soft winds create

as when your stars the heavens did up-raise,

for nature seems dull aside your fair trade,

the artisan of our newly crafted world.

I love the way you hold me close,

the way you bind and look with fiery eyes,

my chest trembling as it reaches out to you,

and every throbbing pulse there drifting up,

echoing with yours in a symphony of love.

We pass the reaches of the old clear sea,

where up and down the lofty pinnacles echo

our own deeds, witnessed by none but nature,

as is the essence of this moment in our lives.

Your body melts into the soft, satin sheets,

and your frame seems floating in silken curves

of silvery folds, reflecting clearly in the light

that allows me to look upon my love.

Your presence fills my life with peace,

holding you near with all our love and faith,

holding you close as tears to grief and pain,

showing you virtues of the centuries old,

and giving you up to kindness and care.

LASTING

Your tender lips brush against my own
and find the bond of union deep and strong,
my humble nature sighs at the sight,
and with a sense of wrong, an inward pain.

For my sighs know that I must one day part
with all this good that fate ordained for me,
and my anxious heart asks what I would do
when our words are spent and love has faded.

But as much I fear I cannot answer so,
for my love for you has power to ordain,
the wish, and dread that, should I die,
my mortal purpose will have been spent.

Your memory has never faded
as I look on you, fondly, lovingly,
while the blue skies above you,
our star, like a golden smile,
glancing softly down your visage.

You always knew
the right thing to say
and how to say it.

You did not need
to seek or search,
and there never was
a story better told,
nor a clearer, more
passionate love held,
by one who knew.

Your love for me is like a healing salve,

it is as the wounds of passion feel more fierce,

more fierce than pangs of anguish churn and swell,

yet the old wounds of our world-wandering souls

are always healed anew, stronger than ever before.

It is a dear and happy sight
to see the changing world
converting to a dusky light,
as it reminds me so very dear
those moments of the night
where we will be as one again.

When I looked in your eyes

I let myself think that soon,

the curtain of your lovely brow

would break in tears of thunder.

So I was moved to pluck you away

and take you down to the summer sea,

to bring you soothing drops of calm,

to gently ease your sore distress.

You are as a great sun in a halo of fire,

turning your face and smiling upon the sea,

all night moving like an elegant shadow

accommodating your will, your desire,

and the dream within my heart of dreams

seeming like a cool breeze, passing by.

An inner strength you channel,

and my own soul's purest heat

eternally shall burn for you

with the passion you crave,

which I never can control.

The way you scrunch up your nose,
the cheeky little glint in your ashen eyes,
your playful smile at the sight of sunrise,
all of these things can make me forget
just how easily I could lose you.

The sweep of countless waters breaking
whose melody is rumbling and low,
the silent bard, that walks the leaves,
I hear, and see, and touch her harp
with the sweet music of her art.

I hear her voice, and think of her,
for her honeyed singing is like a cure,
soothing me and my cares away.

You hold me like a drowning man,
your arms around me, firmly pressing
with an iron hold of loving kindness,
and a hand that caresses me, and a kiss
for my lips that tell me I am saved.

Life is light and love is constant,

where beauty is our dwelling-place,

where all joys, in every mood, are shown,

where laughter sings when the heart is sore,

where roses bloom when all hope is lost.

I hear your singing, deep in my dreams
  whispering as of old to me.

Of the happy days when first you came and
  we laughed and danced on the green.

As I knew the deep, azure blue of your eyes,
  meant happiness and love eternal.

Sleeping, lying still and free,

I saw the shadowed walls

of some old mansion rise,

like some vast temple tall and fair

that welcomes all divine

upon its hallowed ground.

There were chambers deep and dim

that glowed with crimson fires,

rich smells of briar and rose,

of exotic wines, oils and spices,

and the couches spread with silk

with softened pillows bright and fine,

where atop it all I saw your image,

ruling over your divine domain.

For all the hours of woe that I have known
have you a spell to make me love again,
a prize that all my bitter rivals miss.

Or have I met, in your enchanted shade
the respite from all my worldly troubles,
a secret that I dare not lose nor share.

I hear your heart beating fast and strong
as you seem to be enraptured with the scene,
your thoughts as ever entwined in glee
with many a touching moment to share,
pulling at my heart to move as yours.

You always knew the right thing to say,
and never missed a chance to say it right.

You never grew less smart in all our time,
with eyes of shadow, and iron will.

You are respite for my weary eyes,

and the way your kisses fall and rise

remind me of flowers you put in your hair,

the way your fingers curl around and grasp,

and how my breath then comes in a rush,

longing for the heat from your rosy lips.

Our twin souls feel as old eternal stars

burning in one everlasting glorious night,

and we'll never be alone for I truly know

so gently we'll ever meet, time and again.

For you are the mistress of my heart, and

as the reaper is to the fruit of the tree of life,

you will always be fated to harvest my love.

In the silver dusk

sitting on the sand-beach,

the two great stars above

in their spirals circling,

sailing over us and the ocean,

shining through the twilight,

mirroring our close union.

I will forever carry you in my heart,

nor do I think I ever can forget you,

for your precious memory is to me more dear

than all the beauty that my eyes can behold,

or all the love that my heart can cherish.

The shadows gently bend across your cheeks,

and pour their balm and essence onto your form,

all the peaceful beauty and harmony of the earth,

gilded upon your neck and throat, reflecting back,

into my eyes as I take you in, capturing a memory,

one I will hold onto dearly when the shadows pass.

In the land of sunshine and of song

we will find our way, my love and I,

and our paths shall forever be one,

passing over all other worldly aims.

I grasp your hand tightly
as we venture into the unknown,
with all one's worldly hearts and hopes
laying softly and sweetly upon one another.

I am thankful for your kindness,
for in my soft dreaming of you
I have been shy, timid and afraid,
even as the world praises my charms.

Yet I dare to say, now that I am yours,
that I have not always been as I seem.

Time will not stop or part our love
and our lives will not cease to be,
for I wait for your hand to guide my way
and feel it as you press on my heart.

The door may shut, the lamp may burn,
but we will not part until we choose.

Love yourself as I do
for I am bound to you,
as I was bound to you
when I was first dazzled
by your starry heaven,
by your rainbow sky,
and my heart beat high,
for I knew a lover's calm.

My love for you has never ended nor ceased,

and I think on your lips, my fairest one,

whose charm is so strong and true,

still wondering when they cast a spell,

if only so I can remember once more,

to mark the day I fell so deeply for you.

The vibrant memory of
    your touch upon my skin,
the blazing sun
    glowing on your cheeks as you,
with rosy mouth
    and rounded slender fingers,
pressed down
    my heart upon your breasts,
until the day
    was done and the winds moaned,
and the breeze
    released us of our passion.

As we then waited in
    the moonlight for the stars to shine,
a softened light
    upon the magic of your fairest form,
laying together again
    under the watchful gaze of the moon.

Love can be tender thing,

a true friend, not a foe,

and if it be shared and real,

the best thing in the world,

is a friend that knows no fear.

CHANGING

The way we climbed the old mountain-top,

the way that never again seems the same,

how cold it was and how damp and wet,

and how we'd fought the morning through,

and how our little sausage dog stayed true.

How glad we all were of our own,

and how our hearts would open wide,

to hold each other dear and fall in love.

With cold and stalwart shapes, you and I

are alone with life's own searching emptiness.

So let it be, for though our souls may wander

and air be quenchless where our hearts grew

in love and hope, they are not void of being.

My life bleeds through my veins to hear you sigh,

for the world is kinder, but I find it worse,

and I dream of the years that are long past.

The years that I would change, I would live again,

I would relive them, I would dream them all,

yet I would never change you, even if I were to die.

Our love was strong,

Our words bore weight,

Our hopes were bright,

Our eyes were clear,

Our lips were full,

Our words were kind,

Our hearts were pure,

Our hearts were true.

We knew nothing
of what was to come.

We echo deeply, our souls bound,

and in our hearts the tears of pain

rise like to clouds, until the earth

rings with the passing of the night.

Thus we have died, held hand in hand,

the solemn sounds of that great doom

breaking on the grave where there we lie,

both dead and cold, at peace, at one.

The kisses that brought us close,

the stars that your love made plain,

I would have made a forest of them,

I would have made a kingdom of you,

I would have given my heart for you,

had I not lost all my moral strength.

A noble love till one brave heart

forgot its pledge, and fled from us.

We roamed across the foreign seas,

we fought on burning sand, until,

with love dying in our embraces,

we wept together one last time.

When I think of love's deep story

I go back to when I was young,

when I knew that all was good,

that no one sat alone in judgment,

and that she who made up the scale

made no mistake made on her part.

My love for only you, came, and my bliss

saw you in it, and smiled and knew the rest,

that even if my very mortal soul be gone,

my heart would ever remain in your care.

There's a sadness and a joy
in your dear bottomless eyes,
on whose mild, pure surface fall,
the soft and delicate light of love.

I trust that mine and your joy

shall still be bound unto the same,

for it would not be enough that all

our pleasures should be perfect still,

that each should have their gift and care,

and all our lives are one pure delight.

Her eyes were the golden gates of heaven,

her lips as red as any glass of wine,

yet her forehead was suffused with sorrow,

faint with the thoughts that ache the most,

the thoughts that never truly fade away,

the doubts I tried to drown with my love.

Deep in my heart the wounds and the scars
of the old battles we both had to fight.
There was no parting, and no ill-gotten pain.

We woke to find the first rose-bloomed day
had once bloomed again, and that all our days
were each as if themselves one full year of sunshine,
for this was the gift your kindness gave to us.

Her eyes night and day,
her body light and frail,
she was truly beautiful,
she was an angel.

But all at once the lips
that I had dreamed so true
were quiet, softly sobbing.

I kissed her cheek,
I held her in my arms,
and then she was gone.

I hear the steps of a woman, moving

in the place where I used to dwell alone.

I hear the breath of the dawn returning

as the wild heart of the night from the sky

breaks like a spear through the heavens.

With your dear lips and your cheeks so pale,

your brows ripe with the bloom of the spring,

and your kind soul resilient, amid all the woe

the years bring us, like the melody that you sing,

closer together in our ever-growing love.

You my beloved will not leave me here alone,

the night winds will not bear you so far away,

or the pale moon give to you a lorn farewell

from her nightly courts in the heavenly clime.

They will bring the calm and the good again,

and bring back in the dark, your moonlit face.

Your lips so smooth against my cheek

and your shadow lingering in my mind,

as I turn my face and feel your breath

for the kiss that lands to make me yours,

only for your spectre to softly fade away.

She saw me all my life

on the verge of my prime,

I, who in a dream-addled year

languished with laboured breath,

giving up common life and toil

if only to gaze at her eyes,

to feel her touch upon me,

to make her happy again.

A sorrowful time we spent together

while we were on the ocean's waves,

and when you came back again to me

I never knew of such pure content,

and now, if you have lost your way,

know that I am here for you again.

Your slender hands unfold the curtain,
and as soft as twilight, all the windows
fill with the slumbering stars, that warm and still,
hang like silken leaf-drops from a celestial ceiling,
watching over us as we lie together one last time.

She always kept her promises true,

her big blue eyes peppered with joy,

and she never smiled with any doubt

or wept alone in secret, for she knew

that if she had a thought to hide,

it was not one on which to dwell.

All the winds were mute, and on my lonely heart,

the freedom of the forest rose in beauty clear.

You were the only living thing that ever moved

so gracefully, to give me such bliss beyond compare.

Come back to me my love
to heal my hurt when you are gone,
and if this should fail, or seem too hard,
then only a little more will do.

When the tears have ceased to flow

and the thoughts have ceased to be,

we who are left in our sorrow, pray,

pray for the bitter pain to disperse,

for we still remember those we love,

the way we laughed and cried as one.

The light of your smile on the sky

and the shadows of your tears in the grove,

though they mock at the musings I hold most dear,

though they mock at the thoughts that dwell in my soul,

there is no sorrowful, empty, or void-darkened place

that can stand between you and my loving heart.

Remember that hour, the fever,
the fever of that July night
shrivelled into deep slumber.

Yet with two little words
the night was over.

We had walked alone
out of the great town,
where all was still
and dark and dim.

XX
—

A lovely rose that long ago

I loved in summer when the sky was clear.

Now summer is no more

but my heart still grows warm within me,

knowing our bond is not forgotten.

Pressing upon your shadow like a cloak,
enmeshing the spots where your eyes tread,
and with the noblest threads of my life
all wrapped in a mantle of yours,
I may finally be at peace, at last.

The white flowers of heaven at your reddened lips,

in your hands, like snow-flakes, bare and trembling,

with the moon and stars reflecting in your eyes.

That was our blossoming year, with the roses

and the lilies, as fair as their loving queen.

How soft the moonlight
shone on the rocks and sand,
as my heart lay sad and heavy
with dreams of the days to be.

Then in the silence of that unclothed night,
we shared our dreams, our dark secrets too,
we sat around the fire, and wept, and cried,
replaying the daunting beauties of our past.

As you gaze upon me

my words feel so lost,

and you'd have the right

to pity me, as one who had

never known the joys of living.

My eyes suck tears as I see you,

yet my hands are full of you,

for I am drowning in you

as though you are mine,

like flowers that seem

to slowly fade away.

When last I saw you

I was young and bold,

and my heart was fully

set upon our love,

but your fierce spirit,

like frozen waters, rolled

through the calm spring

of my being, and burned

in tumultuous passion,

like the sun-burned flame

that drives men to madness,

to utterly lose themselves.

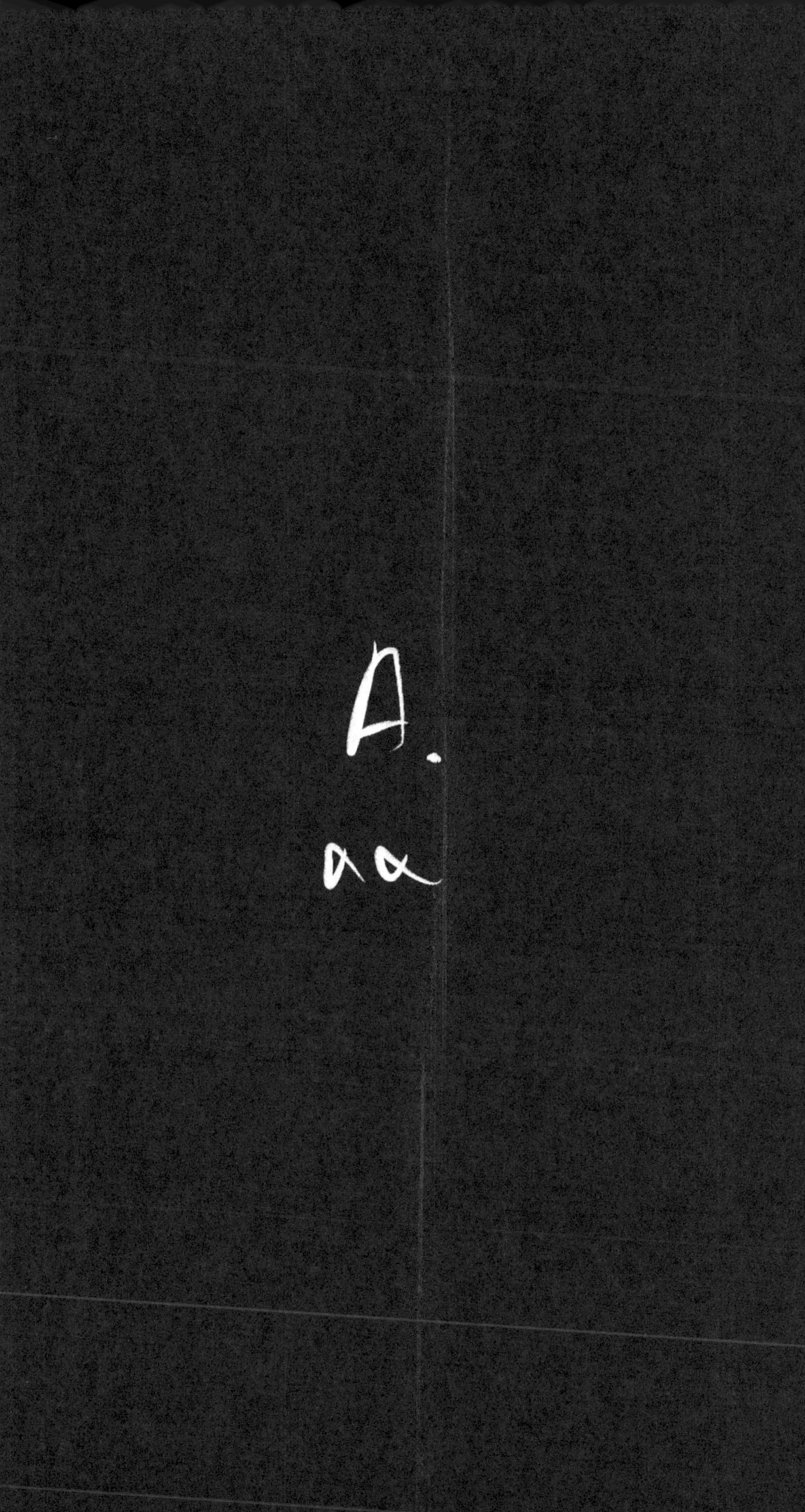